Gun T RPO
Supplemental Material

Copyright: Kenny Simpson
All rights Reserved
ISBN: 978-1-7351591-2-6

Introduction

 # Introduction

I, like most coaches, have worked hard to listen to people I respect and attempt to take little nuggets from those willing to give. Now I have the opportunity to give back, and I hope this offensive system can be of help to you in your journey as a coach. Feel free to take any part of this offense that can help you, but I feel what makes it work is the entire system.

We have worked hard to continue to grow it and work through the problems that can come from blending different worlds.

The entire system can be found on Coachtube.com: https://bit.ly/GUNTRPOSystem

There is also more information on my website: FBCoachSimpson.com.

 # Introduction

This is version 2.0 of the Gun T RPO system. For those of you who may not be familiar with my situation, I developed this system while at Southside Batesville, a 4A school in Arkansas from 2016-2019. This past off-season I had the opportunity to move to Searcy High School, a 6A school in Arkansas.

Searcy had been successful for several years in the spread, so as I took the position we evaluated different aspects we would keep from their system and weave into the Gun T RPO system. While we are still very much a work in progress, there have been several parts that I have added and adjusted to the system. It has been a very fun challenge for me at a higher level of football, and I look forward to continuing to develop as a coach. I hope you gain something from this book, but if you only gain this statement it was worth your purchase:

"Never stop growing as a coach." - I love the thrill of learning and studying football, almost as much as actually coaching the game. When you feel you have nothing new to learn, I'd recommend you find a new profession. The passion we must bring with us is what our athletes deserve from us.

 # Introduction

There is no magic pill. When we watch the game of football there are champions that run a variety of offensive systems. I would point out that those who seem to have the most success have a belief in their offense. Most have worked hard to go over as many "if-then" situations and build in answers. I am no different. I wanted to create an offense that would work against any coverage, any front or any blitz package the defense might throw at us. While the game is won and lost with the players on the field, I wanted to be sure to give my players every advantage I could.

When I first "stepped into the deep end" by putting my offensive system out there, I was overwhelmed by the support from the coaching community. Thank you to the many who have supported me through the past seasons and I look forward to continuing in this world as long as I can be of assistance.

Recommendations

Quotes

"Coach Simpson shows how you can evolve your system to fit your personnel. Too often coaches will as Coach Simpson put it 'try to pound the square peg in the round hole.' Coach's system is one of the best I have seen in my 30 years of coaching, Gun-T 2.0 is an evolution of the system that shows the versatility to adapt to the ever changing kids we see at the high school level." – Matt Bartley

"As a first year head coach and a first time offensive play caller, I don't know where we would have been without the material that coach Simpson has available. We went from 4-6 to 7-4, to the third round of the postseason, and earned the second best record in school history. The program hadn't been to, nor won a playoff game since 2015. Thank you coach Simpson."
-Mike Granato, Head Football Coach, West Orange High School, Florida

"I've been following coach Simpson for a while now and it's very clear to me that even though I may not be a HC, we have similar philosophies. If you are a Wing T guy looking for ways to "Modernize" your offense, or a Spread guy looking for an effective and efficient run game this is the offense you should be looking at!"
Coach Sheffer

Quotes

"The Gun T RPO System really helped us evolve our wing T offense and really put defenses in conflict. This system helped us break a 20 game losing streak and finish with a winning record for the first time since 2014."
-Tom Mulligan, Head Coach Elmwood Park High School, Elmwood Park, New Jersey

"Coach Simpson has modernized the under center Wing-T offense through RPOs, Tempo and outside the box thinking into the explosive Gun-T offense. His courses and books break down the offense into digestible chunks and provide the answers to the most frequent problems you will encounter while running the offense. Coach Simpson is also a class act and is always willing to help out."
-Will Theobold, OC/OL Park High School, Cottage Grove, MN

"Coach Simpson does an awesome job explaining his system, and he does it a way that people like myself who are not familiar with RPOs can understand!"
Coach Coleman

Quotes

"Coach Simpson does a phenomenal job of teaching this dynamic system. He starts from the foundation and works his way through in detail. Coach Simpson gives you the details; yet keeps it simple and efficient just like his offense." - Lucas Stanton

"Over the past year, I have purchased a number of items from Coach Simpson ranging from books to coaching materials. I couldn't be more satisfied with the content and detail of these items. Coach Simpson is a forward thinker and an innovator in this game. Whether you are a young coach or a seasoned veteran there is something for everyone."
-Mike Kloes, Offensive Line Coach, Wahama High School

"Wanting to add modern shotgun style play to your Wing-T system? Coach Simpson has created the definitive playbook combining classic Wing-T elements with modern spread RPO philosophies. A must buy for any Wing-T coach looking to expand their repertoire."
-Tim Jacobs, Head Football Coach, Rex Putnam High School, Milwaukie, Oregon

Table of Contents

Acknowledgements	15
Theory	19
Calling Plays	23
Personnel Decisions	27
Power of Tags	33
-Buck	37
-Counter	45
-Snag	52
New Concepts	57
-Duo	59
-Quick Buck	65
New Formations	71
-Mustang	78
-Empty Dubs	101
-Pro	107
-Triangle	119
-Roar/Lion – Flop	129
If-Then	137
Conclusion	145
About the Author	148

Acknowledgments

Acknowledgements

When I became a football coach many years ago, I wanted to study the game as much as possible. I was very fortunate to have several coaches that served as mentors throughout my career. I also found several coaches that were putting out information before it became "normal". I am thankful for all the guys that were willing to put their system out there.

I started my career as a huge Tony Franklin fan. Then I moved to Rick Stewart about 7-years ago. I wanted to blend these systems. But these coaches, as well as several others, were the pioneers. I want to thank all these coaches who guided me along the path.

I also want to thank those coaches I have worked with during my time at Madison Academy, Alabama Christian Academy, Southside and now Searcy. Coaches are only as good as their staff and I have been part of some great ones and now am leading another very talented staff.

I'd like to also thank my administration at Searcy for the tremendous support this season, and to all the other administrations I've had the honor of serving in my career.

Acknowledgements

Coaches also recognize that the players are the key to the game, and I have been blessed to coach some of the finest young men in the country. The relationships I have with them are more precious than any win. Coaching is a hard, demanding, but truly rewarding profession.

Most importantly my family has been the rock that has always been there for me. My children are now becoming young adults and it is flying by. My wife has been my #1 supporter since day one. She has been through 0-10 seasons as well as through championship seasons, yet she has never wavered.

Theory
Gun T RPO System

Theory

The Gun T RPO system is the best of 3 worlds:

The Wing-T offensive system has been around for many years. The best part of the Wing-T is the run game that utilizes angles and takes advantage of the defensive alignment by creating them. The Wing-T is also known for its "series" based offense, which has multiple plays that look the same in the backfield action.

The RPO system has taken football by storm over the last couple of decades. To be able to place defenders in "conflict" with the run/pass option game gives the offense a numbers advantage at all times. This system is also great because while it seems the quarterback must make a decision on each play, it also "shrinks" his world by having him read only one or two defenders.

The Power-Spread game is gaining steam throughout every level of football. To be in the shotgun, but still have a downhill running game is deadly and difficult to defend. Utilizing tight ends and H-backs has become "new" again in football. The reality is this system has been around for awhile, just not in the shotgun.

Theory

When combined into the Gun T RPO system, these worlds at first seem at odds with one another. However, after a deeper dig, these offenses are all concept based that build in answers to handle any defense that may show up on a given day.

This entire offense is based on answering the "If-Then" question that must be answered. A good defense will have multiple problems it presents to the offense, and your system must have built in answers. Hopefully, through reading some of this material it may provide answers.

Theory

R.P.O. stands for Run-Pass-Option.

In this offense the "R" comes first. We are trying to protect our base run game by supplying answers to problems. The RPO portion of the offense is to build-in answers to protect the running game.

This offense has 1st/2nd/3rd level RPO's. My suggestion to those of you new to this portion of the game would be to start with 1st level RPO's, slowly progress to 2nd, and then possibly 3rd level RPO's.

The beauty of the RPO game is that you can attach the SAME RPO concepts to the entire running game series. Once the quarterback learns the read he can work it on buck sweep or strong belly.

Each of our RPO's is built to address problem areas. We want to have very quick concepts we can go to in the middle of a game. The RPO section is put in with Buck Sweep and Strong Belly and will give you simple RPO concepts that affect the least amount of players (generally the quick tackle and backside players). This allows the offense to become very good at the base run plays with minimal time spent on the backside adjustments.

Calling Plays

Calling Plays

Play call from the coach to the players will follow this format:

1 - Formation (+any tags)
2 - Any motion/shift
3 - Run Concept (+any tags)
4 - RPO Playside
5 - RPO Backside

These can get wordy if you run multiple movements and RPO's on each side, but many plays can be just three words. The only player who needs to learn the entire call is the quarterback.

*As you can see throughout this playbook it will be filled with our base run and pass concepts. But you can be as creative as possible. If I listed every possibility this playbook could easily be well over 400-pages.

Calling Plays

Play call examples –

Red – Buck – Bubble
We would be in "red" formation. The run play would be "buck" and the RPO would be "bubble".

Red – Lion – Belly – Fast
Formation would be "red-lion" (or trips). Run play would be "belly" and the RPO/Screen would be "fast screen".

Red – Empty – Fly – Buck – Bubble
Formation would be Red-Empty. Motion would be "fly" or F motion. Run play would be "buck" and the RPO would be bubble screen.

*More of these play calls are available in the Gun-T-RPO playbook

Personnel

Personnel Choices

When running this offense there are a few "non-negotiable" parts you absolutely must have. But most of the time there are player with the required skills at each position. As I mentioned in a prior chapter, as coaches we must adapt our offense to the players we have. That being said, there are a few qualities you should search for at each position.

Quarterback - This is the key to your offense. Ideally, this position would be a dual threat. While not everyone has that option, he must be at least able to pull the ball from time to time at the very least. The offense will drastically adapt to his skill set. If he is a thrower, it has multiple passing schemes/play action and of course RPO plays. If he is a runner, there are several designed runs for him and the ability to go Empty is a must in today's game.

In short, find your best athlete if possible that can handle the pressure of playing QB and adapt to what he does well. If given the option, I've always deferred to the guy that can run the ball and use his legs over a traditional QB. However, you can be successful with both.

Personnel Choices

F - This should be your best athlete. By design this position will touch the ball the most of any spot (except the QB position). It is easy to get them the ball in space (empty/screens) or simply run the ball (buck/belly). As with every position, you must adapt to their skill set, but this needs to be your best player.

B - This is the hardest position to find and the most important one. It will cause you to adjust what you do offensively to fit his skill set. I attempt to find your second best player if he is able/willing to block and put him in this position. Size will matter at this spot, since he will be asked to down block defensive ends and linebackers. If he is gritty, but undersized, there are some adjustments that can be made, but he must be effective at blocking.

The second part of his job is as important. We want this player to be a good runner – if he is very athletic, we will run jet and counter with him. He also needs to be able to catch at least short passes or play action passes. In my opinion, other than the QB, this position will dictate how much you use certain formations and plays.

Personnel Choices

A – A traditional slot WR. Often for us this is our third RB or an undersized WR. Can get him the ball on multiple concepts and even hand him the ball if you need to.

X – Traditional WR. Depending on what you have available this position can be utilized often, or not much.

Y – Tight-end. Must be able to block defensive lineman. His job is crucial on buck. We generally pick our 3rd guard for this spot. If he has the ability to catch the ball that is great, but he must be a willing and able blocker for this offense to work.

QG – Most important lineman on the team. He needs to be your most athletic player on the line. Size is secondary. He will be pulling on almost all strong side runs. When you decide who goes where, start at this position.

SG – Second most important lineman on the team. He will pull kick most of the time, but needs to be athletic enough to wrap for Quick Belly. Usually the stronger, not as athletic of the two guards.

Personnel Choices

QT – Next most important lineman. What his skill set brings to the table will allow you (or not) to run to the quick side and all your RPO game on the backside. He also needs to be able to get in space on screen and get to second level on RPO game.

C – Must be very consistent at snapping for the offense to run smoothly. Usually this is a smart kid that can call the fronts and is able to handle backside blocking. If he is not as great a blocker, we can give help, but if he is a solid blocker it makes the scheme much easier to achieve.

ST – Usually this is a very physical, but not as athletic tackle. Often for us this is our biggest lineman. If he played at the college level he would have to play guard since often these types of bodies struggle with speed. Must be able to down block, double team and cut/hinge on backside runs.

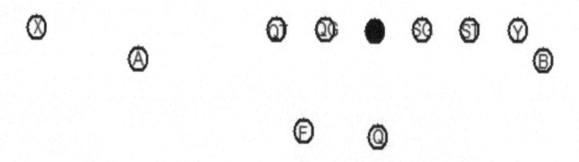

Personnel Choices

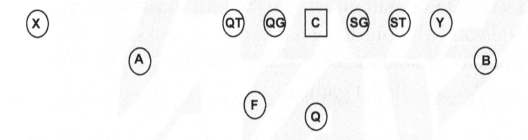

Position	Alignment
X	Top of the numbers
A	Split X and QT off the ball
F	Heels on QB toes. Split the QG and QT
Y	Head even with hip of center. 2 ft splits
B	2x2 off Y
QT	Head even with hip of center. 2 ft splits
QG	Head even with hip of center. 2 ft splits
C	On Ball
SG	Head even with hip of center. 2 ft splits
ST	Head even with hip of center. 2 ft splits
Q	Heels at 5 yards

Power of "Tags"

The Power of "Tags"

The main idea that I have attempted to teach with my kids is "concepts". I want them to understand what we are trying to accomplish in our base run game and pass game concepts. Once they have learned the basic version, this allows us to not only use formations to gain an advantage, but it also allows us to run many of the same plays and "tag" a player we either want to adjust his block/route or even who gets the ball.

I will attempt to go over a few of our concepts we do this with using buck sweep and one of our trips concepts in passing. What has helped our offense is the ability to do this with every running play and every passing concept. While it is important you teach your athletes the base rules on each play and how to run them correctly, as a coach don't ask athletes to do something they are not physically able to do. We must be sure to have the ability to adjust quickly, in our system we call these "tags".

While I have an entire book written dedicated to this one principle https://www.amazon.com/dp/1735159115, here are some tags we have in our offense to help our players. With these tags and RPO checks, we feel we are giving our athletes the opportunity to be successful in our offense.

The Power of "Tags"

As coaches, we must give our athletes a quick adjustment to allow them to be successful when they go against very talented opponents. While we spend 90% of our time teaching the fundamentals and the base way to run each play, we want to be sure to work adjustments.

This offense is also predicated on "if-then" answers. **If** the problem is "X" **then** the answer is "Y". We want each play to have the ability to be successful no matter the look we may get on a Friday night – the power of the "tag". By simply adjusting a blocking assignment or a route we can give the defense issues. This ONLY works if your athletes know the base concept of the play well first. Do not simply tag routes/blocking adjustments without teaching why you are doing so.

The Power of "Tags"

In this section I will just use three base plays we put in and a few examples of how "tags" can make these plays look different or attack different areas of the defense. This is not new material, but the thought process behind the "why". Calling plays should have a system behind it and making adjustments within your own system should be simple for the coach and the players.

Buck
Base Rules

Position	Job Description
X	
A	
F	Cross QB's face for 2 steps, find quick guard and get hand on his back
Y	Gap/Down/Backer
B	Gap/Down/Backer
QT	Step Hinge or Cut
QG	Pull Wrap
C	On/Backside
SG	Pull Kick
ST	Gap/Down/Backer
Q	

Buck Playside Tags

"Bypass"
Tells B leave the 9
Kick out on 9

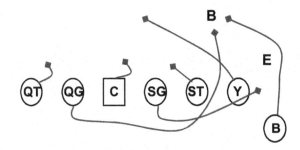

"Dubs"
Tells Y and B to double team
Y vertical push
B horizontal push
Work to backside backer

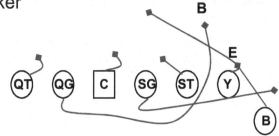

Buck Playside Tags

"Stay"
A and B gaps covered or threatened
C and SG block Down
QG has kick out

"Switch"
SG and ST Switch Jobs

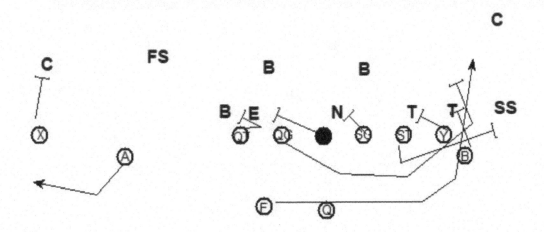

Tags for Buck

Flop – Train Buck - Bubble

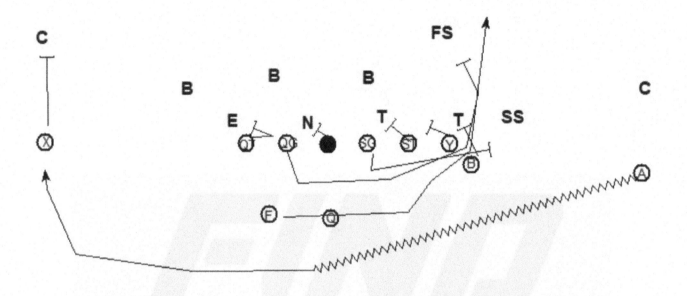

Empty – Fly - Buck

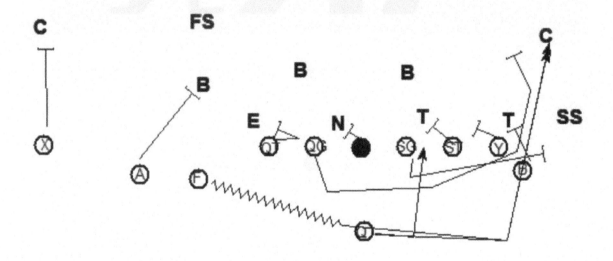

Tags for Buck

Strong – Train Buck

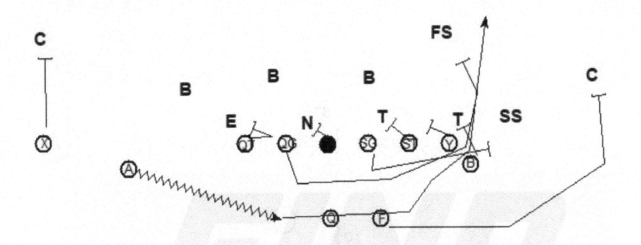

Empty – Q Buck - Bubble

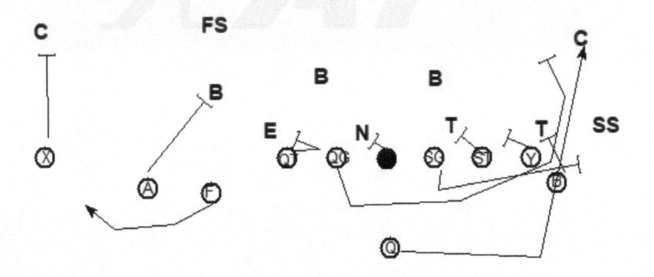

RPO's off Buck

"Peak"
A Works inside leverage, X a Post. QB Reads ILB

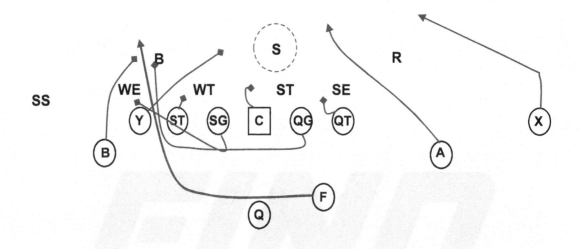

"Key"
Can throw fast screen (A steps on toes of "X" and blocks Most Dangerous). Post snap QB reads ILB for a run

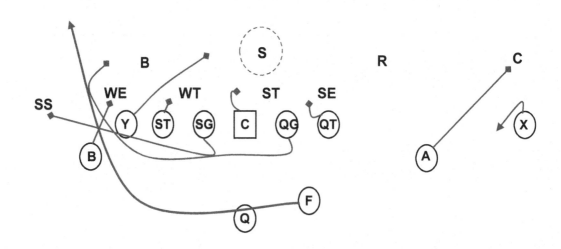

RPO's off Buck

"Read and Bogo"
QB reads the 5 tech. Can throw bubble post snap

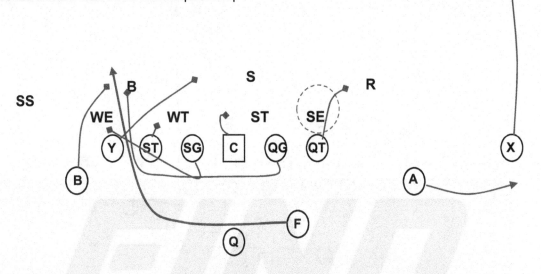

"Steal"
QB reads the 4i/3 tech

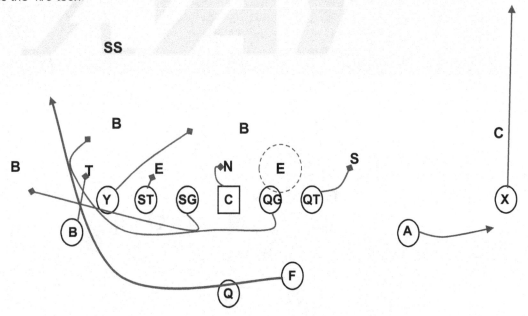

Play Actions off Buck

Flop – Y/B Scissors

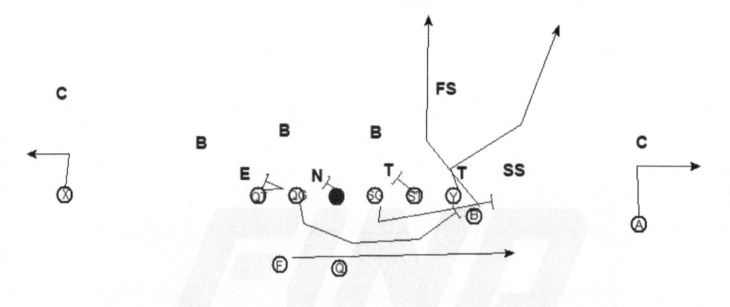

Crack and Go

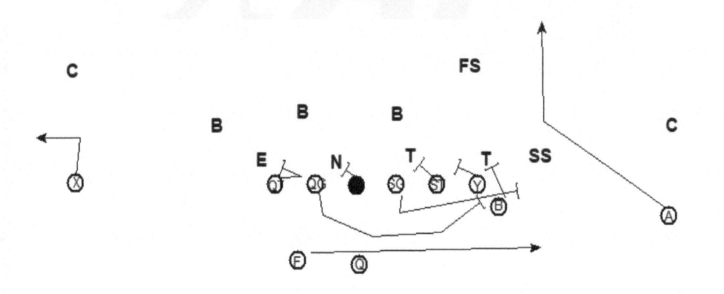

Counter
Base Rules

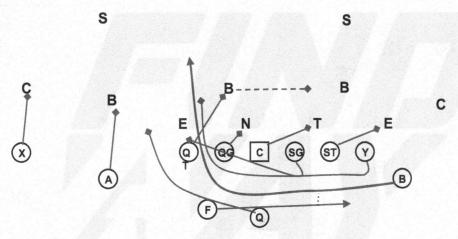

Position	Job Description
X	Block #1
A	Block #2
F	"Take" ball and give underneath carry fake
Y	Pull Wrap
B	Counter and depth step, get ball under F
QT	Gap/Down/Backer- Work path, if playside backer flys out, don't chase, take backside
QG	Gap/Down/Backer
C	Gap/Down/Backer
SG	Pull Kick
ST	Step Hinge
Q	Give ball and block edge

Playside Tags for Counter

"LOCK"
QT blocks out on DE

"STAY"
Y Does not pull – Must Crack with WR's

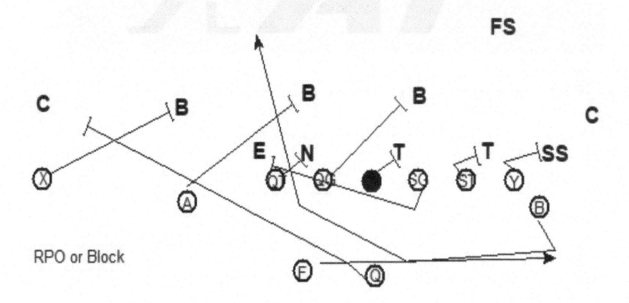

RPO or Block

Playside Tags for Counter

"Switch"
G and T switch roles

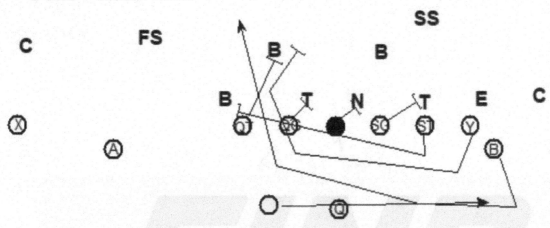

"Keep"
F Keeps the ball – vs. chasing defense

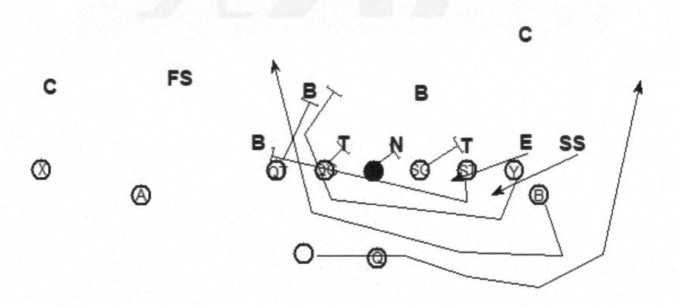

Tags for Counter

Red-Strong-Flop-Counter-Shuffle

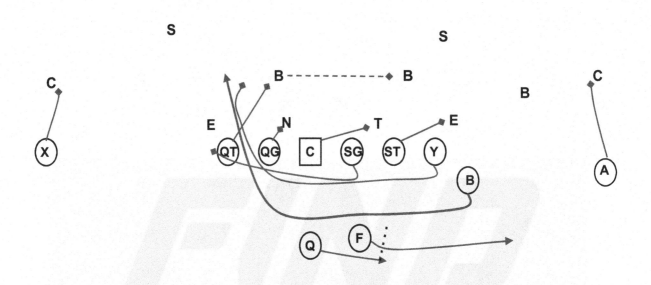

Red-Empty-Counter-43-Bubble
Bubble Presnap

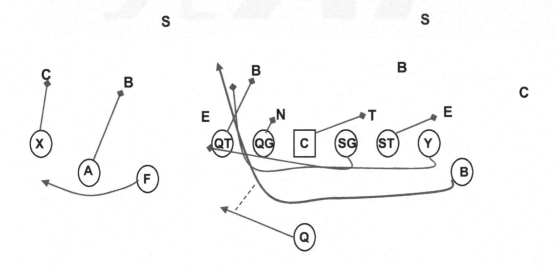

Tags for Counter

Red-Lion-Fly-Q Counter-44
Bubble
Bubble Presnap

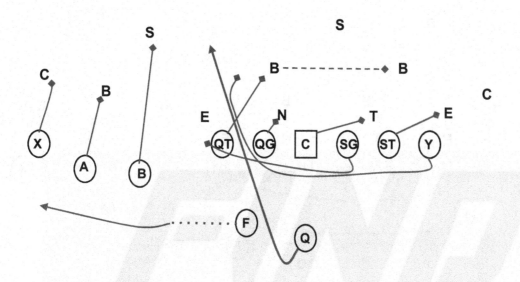

Blue-Counter-Fast
Fast Presnap

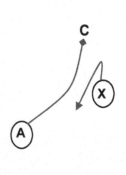

Tags for Counter

Blue-Counter-Fast
Bubble Presnap

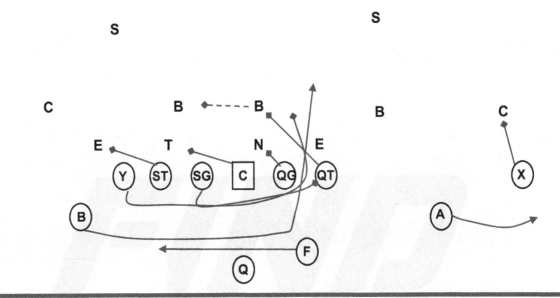

Tags for Counter

"Shuffle"
F runs option path
Q attacks edge then shuttle pass

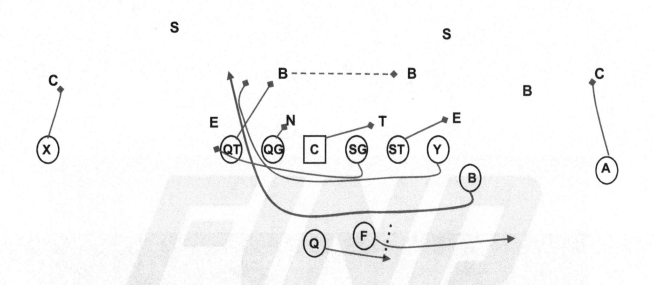

Red-Empty-Counter-42-Bubble
Q read OLB 1st for bubble, then can shuffle if pressure. F crack 2nd level defender. X blocks #1

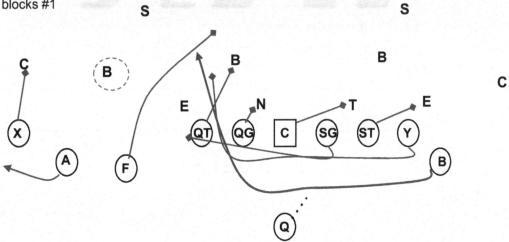

Snag

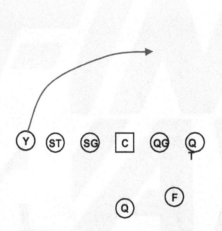
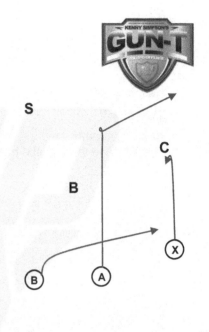

Position	Job Description
X	10-12 yards and get "clear vision lane" to QB
A	Push 7-10, aim for front pylon. QB may bend you
F	Rodeo/Lasso
Y	Drag route over LB. Choke down at hash
B	Chute route-get wide
QT	Rodeo/Lasso
QG	Rodeo/Lasso
C	Rodeo/Lasso
SG	Rodeo/Lasso
ST	Rodeo/Lasso
Q	Attack edge. Read flat defender to deep. B is hot or if flat defender drops

Tags for Snag

Red-Squeeze-Bus-Snag
X outside release to 12 yards
A push to 7 then front pylon

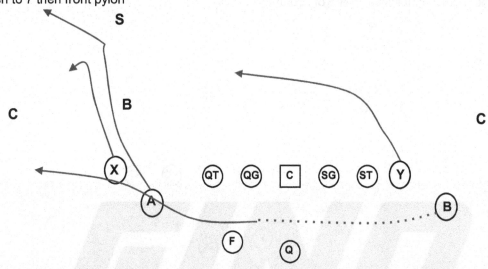

Red-Bus-Snag-A throwback
A work 7-10 and then across gaining depth to 15-20
Can cheat alignment tighter to line of scrimmage

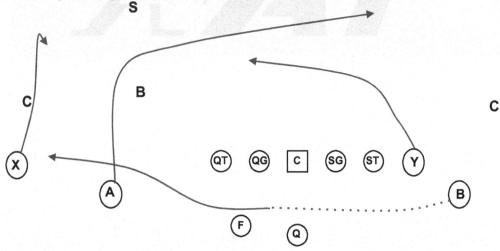

Tags for Snag

Red-Bus-Snag-X throwback

X work 7-10 and then across gaining depth to 15-20
Can cheat alignment tighter to line of scrimmage

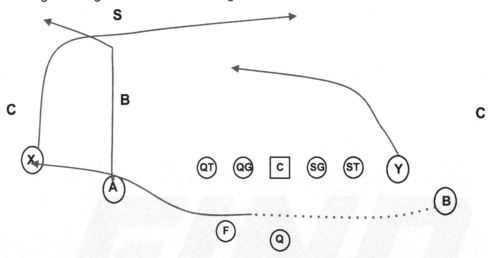

The Power of "Tags"

Those are three of our base plays. We want the ability to be able to run our base offense with very little adjusting – we refer to those as "tags". When you add in tags to your offense it gives it variety and a different look for the defense without complicating things for your players.

IN ORDER TO DO THIS –

1) You must be great at your base way of running each play.

2) The offense must also not have too many concepts or it will become difficult to run tags.

3) Finally, your QB must be able to handle the adjustments.

New Play Concepts

New Concepts

I firmly believe that for an offense to be successful, it must have never changing core values:

1) Have plays built in with a series – play action, rpo, counter

2) Match blocking schemes to maximize value – or use the same terminology so plays are easier to learn and adapt to any front

3) Be sure everything you have in your offense can be done in your base and main formations.

With all that being said, I do believe you must adapt each year to the personnel on your team. This past season I moved to another school and had different type athletes. To that end, our staff looked to find answers in our offense that would match our players.

In this section, I will go over the two major concepts we added into the offense that helped in the run game and a few play action passes that we used to marry with the run game.

New Concepts

DUO or Inside Zone is not something I thought I'd ever fit into our offense...Until I came to a new school that already knew the concept well. After giving it a few token practices to look at, I quickly realized that it gave us a new element in the running game.

We teach this as a Double Team on as many players as possible to second level. It has given us a much more versatile inside run for nights when pulling causes issues, and it also gives defenses issues with trying to read our guards.

In the follow pages I'll go over DUO out of a few formations and against multiple fronts.

DUO
Base Rules

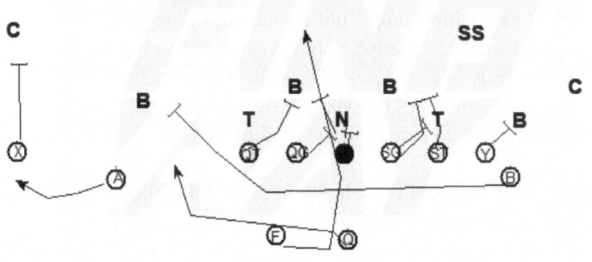

Position	Job Description
X	RPO Concept – Usually Bubble or Fast
A	RPO Concept – Usually Bubble of Fast
F	Slide step to QB – Press Double Team by center and make cut
Y	Block out
B	Cross Line and look for second level backside LB
QT	B Gap Defender – to LB
QG	A Gap Defender – to LB
C	A Gap Defender – to LB
SG	B Gap Defender – to LB
ST	B/C Gap Defender – to LB
Q	Read backside DE out of base

DUO Tags

"Kick"
Tells B Kick out DE

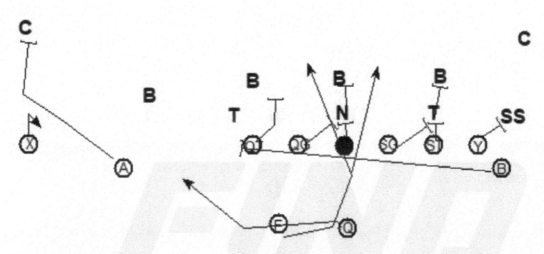

"TUG"
Guard blocks out on DE and Tackle Wraps to LB

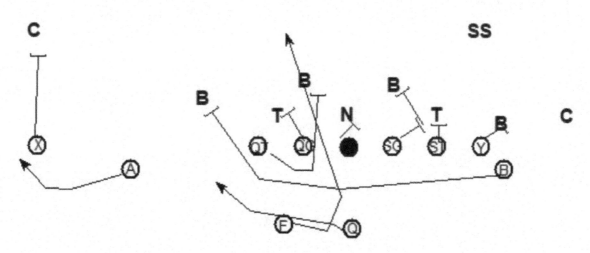

DUO Tags

"Lock"
QT Locks the DE
– B Inserts

RPO Concept

"Lock" - Peak

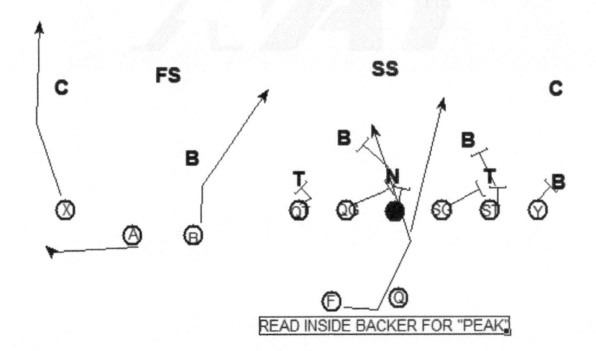

READ INSIDE BACKER FOR "PEAK"

DUO/Inside Zone

4-3

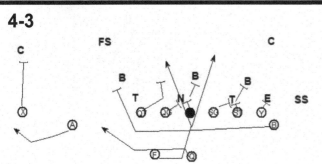

3-3

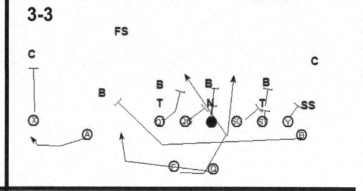

Under

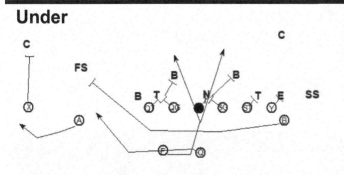

3-4

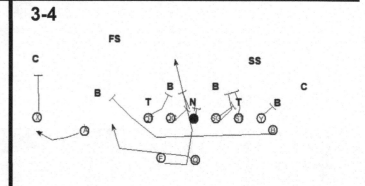

DUO-Pass
Base Rules

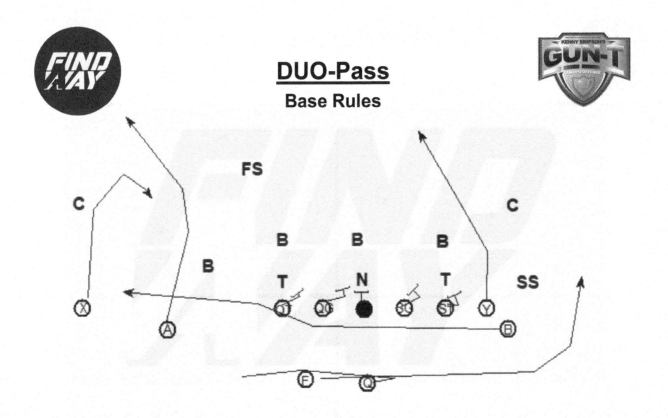

Position	Job Description
X	Curl Route
A	Corner Route
F	Fake Buck – Wheel Late
Y	Post Route
B	Cross Line and get to flats
QT	Step Like Duo
QG	Protect A Gap
C	A Gap Defender
SG	B Gap Defender
ST	C Gap Defender
Q	Ride Back and get width – If OLB crashes or bails throw chute – if not curl/corner

New Concepts

Quick Buck is something I have played with in the past, but have not had as much success as I would have liked. This season we moved to running it much more and with more success than any previous season I have had. It does take some teaching, but if your guards are able to pick up on the concept it is a very good compliment to attack odd front teams or 4 front teams that slant.

We teach cracking with our WR's on most plays, so this is not a new concept for them. I've always believed against man-to-man, the crack block has the potential to block 2 guys with one man. Even if it doesn't succeed, you are generally forcing a corner to make the tackle.

Quick Buck
Base Rules

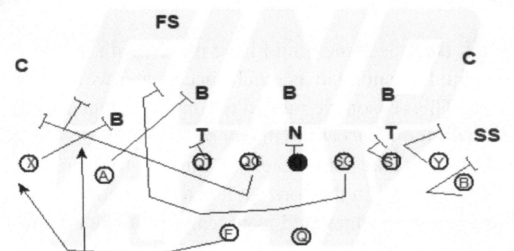

Position	Job Description
X	Crack first second level defender
A	Crack inside linebacker (unless OLB is inside by alignment)
F	Swing pass and follow guards.
Y	Step Hinge
B	Step Hinge
QT	Block DE
QG	Pull Kick/Wrap quick side
C	Cut first defender playside
SG	Pull Wrap – Eyes inside
ST	Step Hinge/Cut
Q	Ball out quickly

Quick Buck Flavors

Mustang – Quick Buck

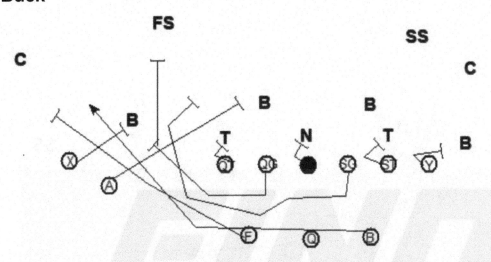

Trips – Quick Buck

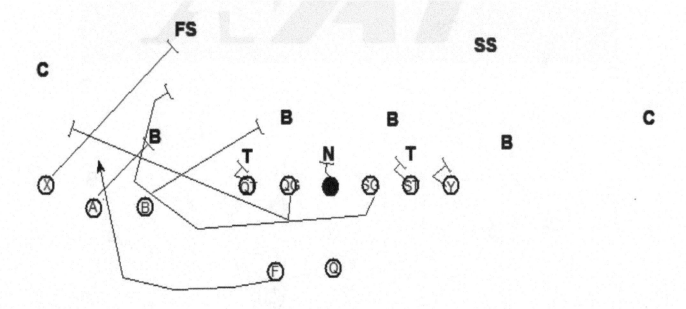

Quick Buck Flavors

QB – Quick Buck

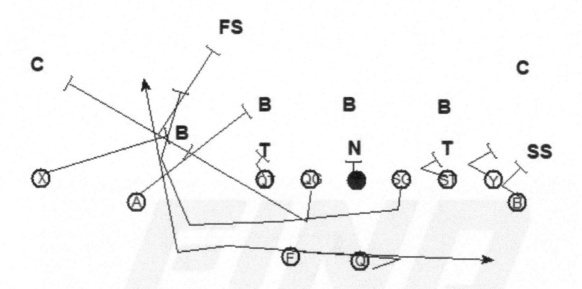

Empty – Bus Quick Buck

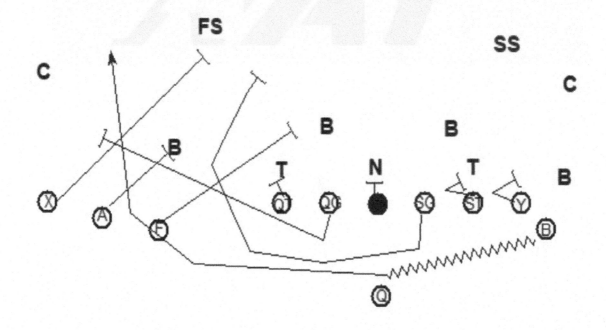

Quick Buck

4-3

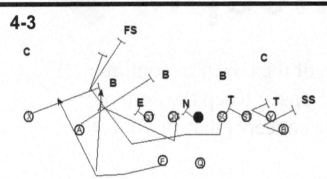

3-3

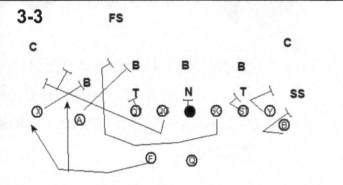

Under

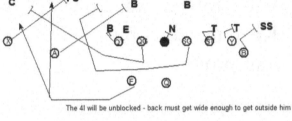

The 4I will be unblocked - back must get wide enough to get outside him

3-4

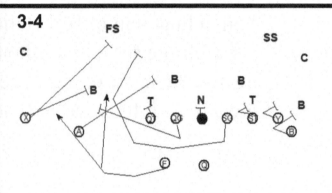

New Concepts

Each year I believe it is the job of the coach to continue to find what will match their offense. Keep the core of the offense, but always look for concepts that fit your athletes.

I am a huge fan of Bill Belichick and what he has done for multiple seasons. Adapting to what you have each year is the mark of a great coach. Keep the core, but always look for what will benefit your program.

Formations

 # Formations

Formations are an area that can be complicated in any offense or sometimes overly simple. Each year I explore a few formations that may give our team an advantage, but I live by the rule – Simple is best. If a team runs too many formations it can be difficult to predict how a defense will react and thus difficult to teach your athletes what to expect. On the flip side, if an offense lives in 1-2 formations the majority of the game, the defense may be able to create multiple looks to attack it with no fear of an answer.

In this section I will share a variety of looks this offense can get into with one or two word tags. I'd caution you as a coach, to be sure you are great at your base, before working these additional formations. Generally, if we are using multiple formations, we are doing so for one of the following reasons:

 # Formations

1) Exploit a weakness we have seen in defensive alignment

2) Attack a player on the defense by getting him isolated

3) Matching personnel with better formations – May have a player that is better in space or not as good in space

4) Move away from stronger players on defense – Get the defense to put best players one place and then go the other direction.

In my previous book I had a very large section of formations. In this 2.0 addition, I will just address some extra formations that may be of help.

Formations

Under each formation I will list a few concepts we use. Again, I want to caution that if you become "formation dependent" (or only run certain plays from certain formations) you will become easier to defend. The goal is to run as many of your base concepts from any formation that is used.

While we do more things from these formations I am going to list and show, it will give you a good idea of how to take these formations and work towards creating matchups that will benefit your offense.

In each section you will find –
1) Base sets and easy tags that fit with base formations
2) Base run/rpo concepts
3) Plays that take advantage of what a defense is giving

Remember, in this offense each play is able to be run from each formation, if the defense gives the look that is desired.

Power of Formations

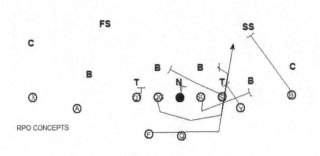

RPO CONCEPTS

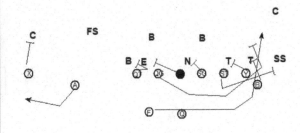

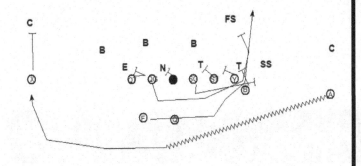

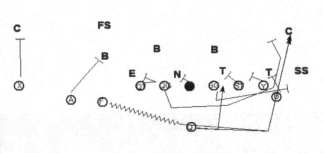

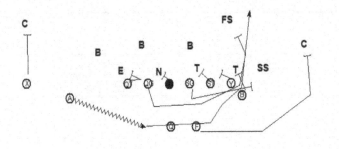

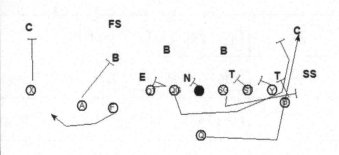

This is Buck Sweep run from multiple formations and from multiple motions. I use this as simply and example of why formations and motions matter in this offense. Running the base play is most important, but being able to motion and use formation gives a great advantage.

Red

Position	Alignment
X	Top of the numbers
A	Split X and QT off the ball
F	Heels on QB toes. Split the QG and QT
Y	Head even with hip of center. 2 ft splits
B	2x2 off Y
QT	Head even with hip of center. 2 ft splits
QG	Head even with hip of center. 2 ft splits
C	On Ball
SG	Head even with hip of center. 2 ft splits
ST	Head even with hip of center. 2 ft splits
Q	Heels at 5 yards

Blue

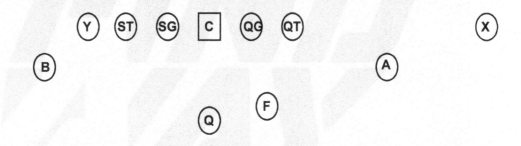

Position	Alignment
X	Top of the numbers
A	Split X and QT off the ball
F	Heels on QB toes. Split the QG and QT
Y	Head even with hip of center. 2 ft splits
B	2x2 off Y
QT	Head even with hip of center. 2 ft splits
QG	Head even with hip of center. 2 ft splits
C	On Ball
SG	Head even with hip of center. 2 ft splits
ST	Head even with hip of center. 2 ft splits
Q	Heels at 5 yards

Mustang

Mustang

Mustang formation was a package we found some success with. It is a way to get two tailbacks on the field together. We were able to run almost all our base offense from this set and while I'd prefer to be able to keep the TE/WING look, this was a help for those teams that may not have a "B" that is able to handle some of the blocking assignments, but is a talented runner.

It is becoming much more utilized at the collegiate level with deeper concepts, but we love it since it can be paired with many of our inside run game concepts.

Red
Mustang

Position	Alignment
X	Top of the numbers
A	Split X and QT off the ball
F	Heels on QB toes. Split the QG and QT
Y	Head even with hip of center. 2 ft splits
B	Heels on QB toes. Split the SG and ST.
QT	Head even with hip of center. 2 ft splits
QG	Head even with hip of center. 2 ft splits
C	On Ball
SG	Head even with hip of center. 2 ft splits
ST	Head even with hip of center. 2 ft splits
Q	Heels at 5 yards

Blue
Mustang

Position	Alignment
X	Top of the numbers
A	Split X and QT off the ball
F	Heels on QB toes. Split the QG and QT
Y	Head even with hip of center. 2 ft splits
B	Heels on QB toes. Split the SG and ST.
QT	Head even with hip of center. 2 ft splits
QG	Head even with hip of center. 2 ft splits
C	On Ball
SG	Head even with hip of center. 2 ft splits
ST	Head even with hip of center. 2 ft splits
Q	Heels at 5 yards

Red
Mustang Flop

Position	Alignment
X	Top of the numbers
A	Top of the numbers off the ball
F	Heels on QB toes. Split the QG and QT
Y	Head even with hip of center. 2 ft splits
B	Heels on QB toes. Split the SG and ST.
QT	Head even with hip of center. 2 ft splits
QG	Head even with hip of center. 2 ft splits
C	On Ball
SG	Head even with hip of center. 2 ft splits
ST	Head even with hip of center. 2 ft splits
Q	Heels at 5 yards

Blue
Mustang Flop

Position	Alignment
X	Top of the numbers
A	Top of the numbers off the ball
F	Heels on QB toes. Split the QG and QT
Y	Head even with hip of center. 2 ft splits
B	Heels on QB toes. Split the SG and ST.
QT	Head even with hip of center. 2 ft splits
QG	Head even with hip of center. 2 ft splits
C	On Ball
SG	Head even with hip of center. 2 ft splits
ST	Head even with hip of center. 2 ft splits
Q	Heels at 5 yards

Mustang

In this section I have shown our base offensive package from "mustang", but just like the rest of the offense, by using tags and shifts it can be as complicated as you'd like to make it look with some "window dressing". We also were able to run most of our base RPO game on the backside with no changes needed.

Several coaches also spoke with me during the off-season about running the quick side without using your QB and this formation makes that simple with Quick Belly/Counter/Jet all very simple to run.

Red
Mustang

Position	Alignment
X	Top of the numbers
A	Split X and QT off the ball
F	Heels on QB toes. Split the QG and QT
Y	Head even with hip of center. 2 ft splits
B	Heels on QB toes. Split the SG and ST.
QT	Head even with hip of center. 2 ft splits
QG	Head even with hip of center. 2 ft splits
C	On Ball
SG	Head even with hip of center. 2 ft splits
ST	Head even with hip of center. 2 ft splits
Q	Heels at 5 yards

Red
Mustang Flop

Position	Alignment
X	Top of the numbers
A	Top of the numbers off the ball
F	Heels on QB toes. Split the QG and QT
Y	Head even with hip of center. 2 ft splits
B	Heels on QB toes. Split the SG and ST.
QT	Head even with hip of center. 2 ft splits
QG	Head even with hip of center. 2 ft splits
C	On Ball
SG	Head even with hip of center. 2 ft splits
ST	Head even with hip of center. 2 ft splits
Q	Heels at 5 yards

Buck
Base Rules

Position	Job Description
X	Same RPO's as in base
A	Same RPO's as in base
F	Cross QB's face for 2 steps, find quick guard and get hand on his back
Y	Gap/Down/Backer
B	Arc to second level defender.
QT	Step Hinge or Cut
QG	Pull Wrap
C	On/Backside
SG	Pull Kick
ST	Gap/Down/Backer
Q	Same RPO's as in base

Belly
Base Rules

Position	Job Description
X	Same RPO's as in base
A	Same RPO's as in base
F	
Y	Block Out
B	Fold inside to playside LB
QT	Step Hinge unless RPO
QG	Wrap to first daylight. Eyes inside
C	On/Backside
SG	#1 Defensive Lineman
ST	#2 Defensive Lineman. If #2 is outside Y, then DBL to backside LB
Q	Same RPO's as in base

Counter
Base Rules

Position	Job Description
X	Block #1
A	Block #2
F	Fake Handoff and block edge.
Y	Pull Wrap
B	Counter step and take ball. Follow Y.
QT	Gap/Down/Backer- Work path, if playside backer flys out, don't chase, take backside
QG	Gap/Down/Backer
C	Gap/Down/Backer
SG	Pull Kick
ST	Step Hinge
Q	Give ball and block edge

Jet
Base Rules

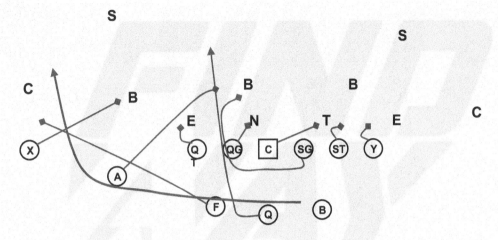

Position	Job Description
X	Crack OLB
A	Chip 5 tech if needed, crack ILB
F	Take flat path and kick first defender to show. If no one shows, wrap to corner
Y	Step inside, hinge
B	Flat on handoff. Cut off F block.
QT	Hook DE
QG	Block #1 DL, Hook 3 tech
C	On/Backside
SG	Wrap through first gap on quickside, eyes inside
ST	Step inside, hinge
Q	Hand or toss to B

Quick Belly
Base Rules

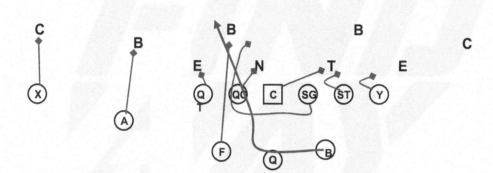

Position	Job Description
X	RPO if no motion. If motion block #1
A	RPO if no motion. If motion block #2
F	Lead on ILB (Play side)
Y	Step in, hinge
B	Slide step and follow F.
QT	#2 DL Block out, if aligned inside, take in
QG	#1 DL
C	On/Backside
SG	Wrap first gap quick side, look inside
ST	Step in, hinge
Q	Turn at 45 and hand to B.

Belly Read
Base Rules

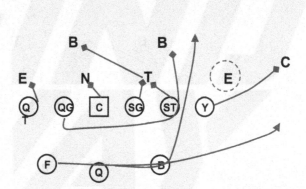

Position	Job Description
X	RPO or Screen
A	RPO or Screen
F	Run flat to edge and follow the Y/B blocks
Y	Block first edge outside read man, try to seal
B	Outside Release and look to seal any alley player
QT	Step Hinge or Cut
QG	Pull Wrap
C	On/Backside
SG	Pull Kick
ST	Gap/Down/Backer
Q	Shuffle 2 steps and read the 1st DL head up the ST to outside

Quick Belly Read
Base Rules

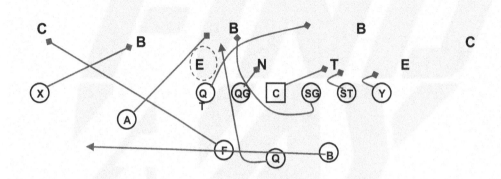

Position	Job Description
X	Crack OLB
A	Crack ILB
F	Kickout #1
Y	Step in, hinge
B	Expect to run jet
QT	Gap, down, backer
QG	#1 DL
C	On/Backside
SG	Wrap first gap quick side, look inside
ST	Step in, hinge
Q	2 shuffles to read

Waggle
Can use Rodeo/Lasso protection

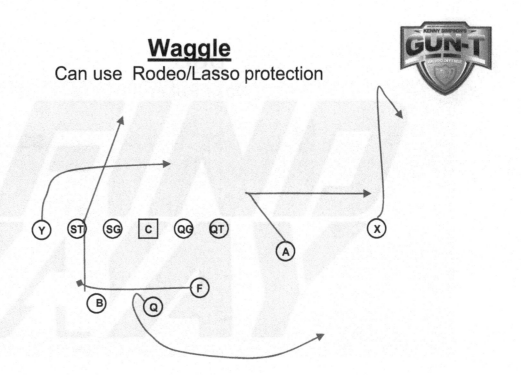

Position	Job Description
X	Smoke route. 16 yards back to 14
A	3 steps inside, break to flat
F	Fake buck and block edge
Y	Drag over linebackers
B	Post over safety – Will get there late.
QT	Down
QG	Down
C	Down
SG	Pull and secure edge
ST	Step and Hinge
Q	Fake and shuffle, get depth. A is hot, X is primary, Y is second

DUO
Base Rules

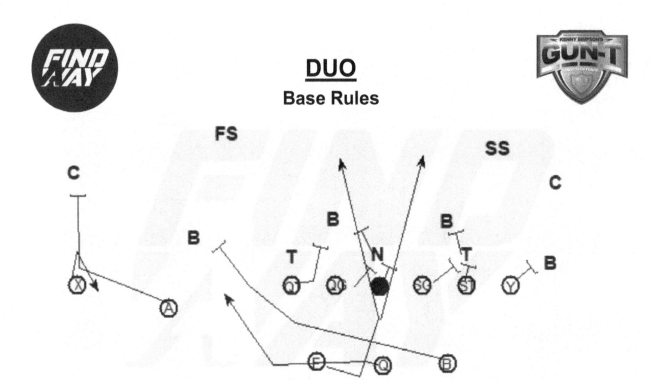

Position	Job Description
X	Fast Screen – Can be another RPO concept
A	Block MDT – Can be another RPO concept
F	Duo
Y	Block Out
B	Wrap to second level LB
QT	B Gap Defender
QG	Double A Gap Defender to LB
C	Double A Gap Defender to LB
SG	Double B Gap Defender to LB
ST	Double B Gap Defender to LB
Q	Read backside DE, Can throw RPO now or after the read

DUO PASS
Base Rules

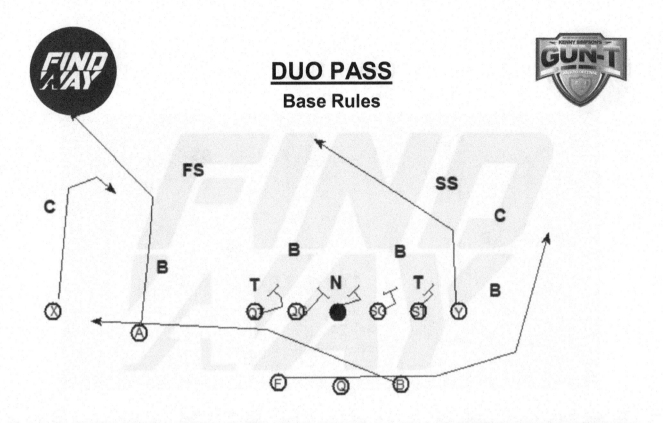

Position	Job Description
X	Curl Route at 10 back to 8
A	Corner Route
F	Fake Buck
Y	Post
B	Fake Kickout block to flats
QT	Duo - Hinge
QG	Duo – Alert (don't go upfield)
C	Duo – Alert (don't go upfield)
SG	Duo – Alert (don't go upfield)
ST	Duo – Alert (don't go upfield)
Q	Fake Duo Attack edge – look at flat defender

Quick Buck
Base Rules

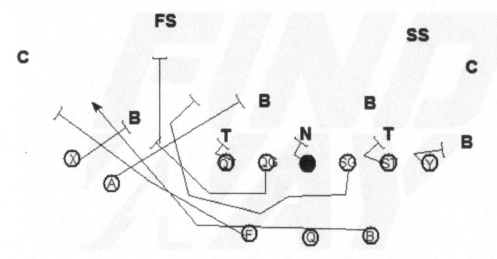

Position	Job Description
X	Crack second level defender
A	Crack ILB
F	Block #1 Outside Defender
Y	Gap-Hinge
B	Run Buck to quick side
QT	Hook/block down on/cut - DE
QG	Pull Kick
C	Cut first defender to playside
SG	Pull – Wrap first daylight – EYES INSIDE
ST	Gap-Hinge
Q	Hand to B – Can read backside if RPO

Counter
Base Rules

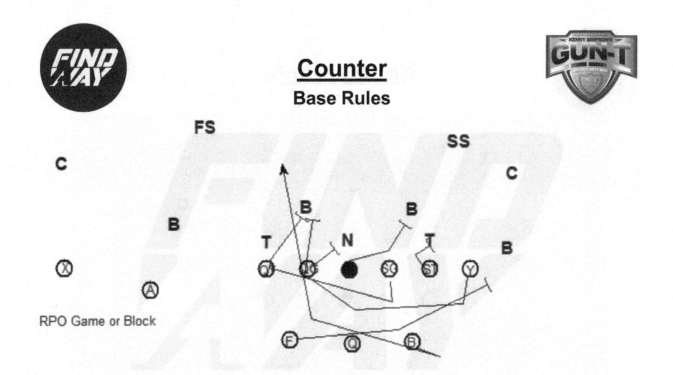

Position	Job Description
X	
A	
F	Fake Buck – Block Edge Defender
Y	Pull Wrap
B	Counter Step out – Crossover and follow the Y
QT	Gap-Down-Backer
QG	Gap-Down-Backer
C	Gap-Down-Backer
SG	Pull Kick
ST	Gap-Hinge
Q	Fake ball to the F and give to the B

Counter Pass
Base Rules

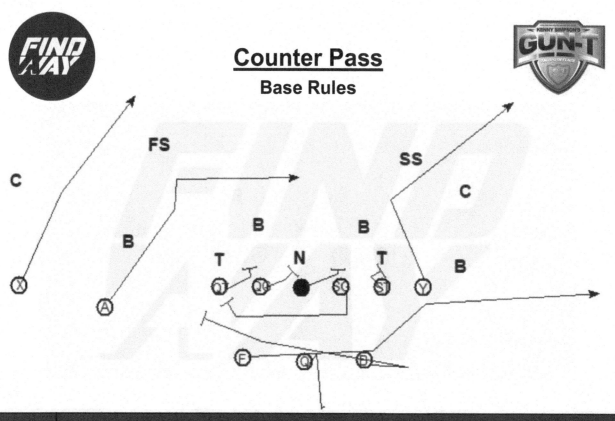

Position	Job Description
X	Post over safety
A	Dig – over the LB's
F	Fake Buck – Run Chute Route
Y	Corner Route
B	Counter Step out – Crossover and block Edge
QT	Gap-Down
QG	Gap-Down
C	Gap-Down
SG	Pull Kick
ST	Gap-Hinge
Q	Fake ball to the F and B – Reading the Safety on playside

 # Empty "DUBS"

One of the elements of our offense in previous seasons that became clear, was that when we went to a more "spread" look it caused multiple problems for the defense:

1) They had to match our athletes if they chose to stay in man-to-man and we could manipulate matchups

2) They often left a very light box and running our base run concepts was much easier

3) The screen game/quick game became simple to tag to a run and we now had a full field RPO

We used this set sparingly this season, but we had success getting what we wanted from it often. An empty set with a TE attached is difficult for a defense to line up against. Especially since we often have a Wing attached to the TE.

 # Empty "DUBS"

The "Dubs" tells our "F" and "B" they will go out to the strong side of the call. In this set the QB can still run all your base run concepts as well. Since it is empty he knows all run calls involve him.

*Recommended use – if you have a QB that can run or you have 4 WR type athletes that can run quick game pass concepts.

Many times in this set you can run a 3-way RPO if the QB could handle it.

Example – Belly (with QB), Screen concept and quick concept

Red
Empty Dubs

Position	Alignment
X	Top of the numbers
A	Split the difference. Heels on toes of X.
F	Split the difference. Heels on toes of Y.
Y	Head even with hip of center. 2 ft splits
B	Top of the numbers. Off the ball.
QT	Head even with hip of center. 2 ft splits
QG	Head even with hip of center. 2 ft splits
C	On Ball
SG	Head even with hip of center. 2 ft splits
ST	Head even with hip of center. 2 ft splits
Q	Heels at 5 yards

Blue
Empty Dubs

Position	Alignment
X	Top of the numbers
A	Split the difference. Heels on toes of X.
F	Split the difference. Heels on toes of Y.
Y	Head even with hip of center. 2 ft splits
B	Top of numbers. Off the ball.
QT	Head even with hip of center. 2 ft splits
QG	Head even with hip of center. 2 ft splits
C	On Ball
SG	Head even with hip of center. 2 ft splits
ST	Head even with hip of center. 2 ft splits
Q	Heels at 5 yards

Belly-Fast-Bubble
Base Rules

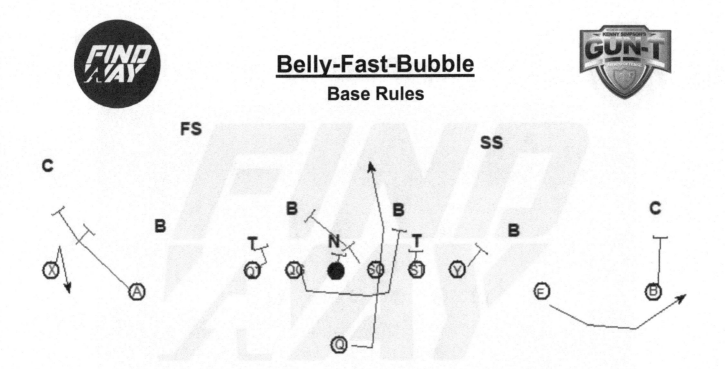

Position	Job Description
X	RPO called first
A	RPO called first
F	RPO called second
Y	Lead on playside LB
B	RPO called second
QT	Step Hinge
QG	Wrap to first daylight. Eyes inside
C	On/Backside
SG	#1 Defensive Lineman inside of the ST
ST	Block Out
Q	Screen Check to QB run

Train-Belly Read
Base Rules

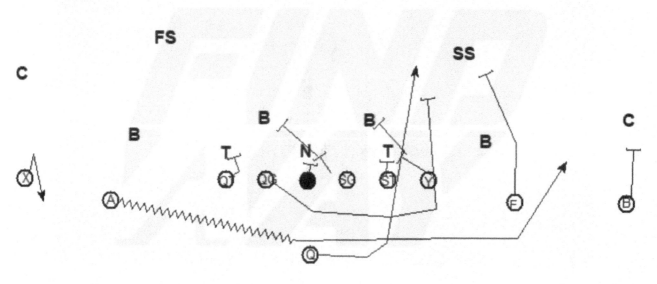

Position	Job Description
X	Route/Screen or block
A	Jet to the strong side
F	Block Safety/ILB – Leave OLB alone
Y	Block Belly Read
B	Block Corner
QT	Step Hinge
QG	Wrap to first daylight. Eyes inside
C	On/Backside
SG	#1 Defensive Lineman inside of the ST
ST	Belly Read
Q	Read OLB

PRO

One area that I feel most teams struggle to find is a wing-back "B" that is able to handle every skill we ask of him. Blocking, running and catching the ball at a high level is a big challenge for many. To combat this, many teams are already working with a set very similar to this and refer to it as "20" personnel grouping. We simply call it "PRO".

Issues you will need to work through for this set:

1) Your TE must be athletic enough to be off the ball, this is a harder block

2) Your "B" must be good enough to win 1 on 1 matchups.

3) Run game adjustments are subtle, but they do break a few rules with your TE.

Benefits of using this set:

1) May get much lighter box and often 2-high look from a defense.

2) Now asking a TE to block bigger players.

3) Can run 3 way RPO game.

Red
Pro

Position	Alignment
X	Top of the numbers
A	Split X and QT off the ball
F	Heels on QB toes. Split the QG and QT
Y	2 x 2 off ST.
B	6-8 Yard split off the Y. On the line.
QT	Head even with hip of center. 2 ft splits
QG	Head even with hip of center. 2 ft splits
C	On Ball
SG	Head even with hip of center. 2 ft splits
ST	Head even with hip of center. 2 ft splits
Q	Heels at 5 yards

Blue
Pro

Position	Alignment
X	Top of the numbers
A	Split X and QT off the ball
F	Heels on QB toes. Split the QG and QT
Y	2 x 2 off the ST.
B	6-8 yard split. On the line.
QT	Head even with hip of center. 2 ft splits
QG	Head even with hip of center. 2 ft splits
C	On Ball
SG	Head even with hip of center. 2 ft splits
ST	Head even with hip of center. 2 ft splits
Q	Heels at 5 yards

Red
Pro Flop

Position	Alignment
X	Top of the numbers
A	Top of the numbers. Toes on heels of B.
F	Heels on QB toes. Split the QG and QT
Y	2 x 2 off ST.
B	6-8 Yard split off the Y. On the line.
QT	Head even with hip of center. 2 ft splits
QG	Head even with hip of center. 2 ft splits
C	On Ball
SG	Head even with hip of center. 2 ft splits
ST	Head even with hip of center. 2 ft splits
Q	Heels at 5 yards

Blue
Pro Flop

Position	Alignment
X	Top of the numbers
A	Top of the numbers. Toes on heels of B.
F	Heels on QB toes. Split the QG and QT
Y	2 x 2 off the ST.
B	6-8 yard split. On the line.
QT	Head even with hip of center. 2 ft splits
QG	Head even with hip of center. 2 ft splits
C	On Ball
SG	Head even with hip of center. 2 ft splits
ST	Head even with hip of center. 2 ft splits
Q	Heels at 5 yards

Buck
Base Rules

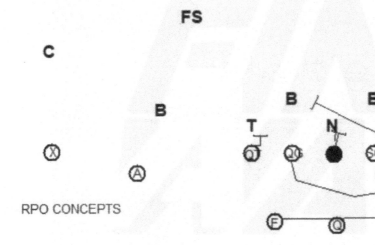

RPO CONCEPTS

Position	Job Description
X	Same RPO's as in base
A	Same RPO's as in base
F	Cross QB's face for 2 steps, find quick guard and get hand on his back
Y	Gap/Down/Backer
B	Crack Safety/ILB if in 3-3 stack
QT	Step Hinge or Cut
QG	Pull Wrap
C	On/Backside
SG	Pull Kick
ST	Gap/Down/Backer
Q	Same RPO's as in base

Belly
Base Rules

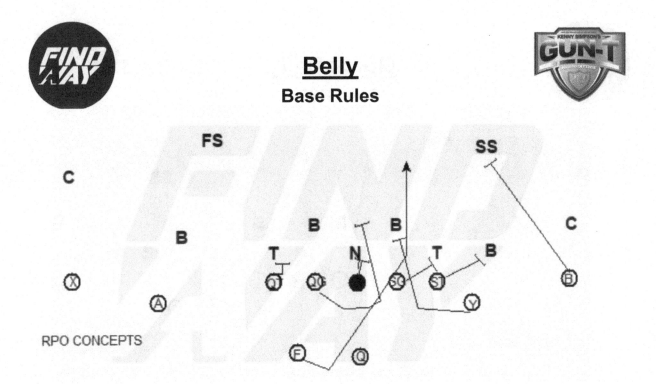

RPO CONCEPTS

Position	Job Description
X	Same RPO's as in base
A	Same RPO's as in base
F	
Y	Lead on playside LB
B	Crack Safety or block corner if single high
QT	Step Hinge unless RPO
QG	Wrap to first daylight. Eyes inside
C	On/Backside
SG	#1 Defensive Lineman inside of the ST
ST	Block Out
Q	Same RPO's as in base

Quick Belly
Base Rules

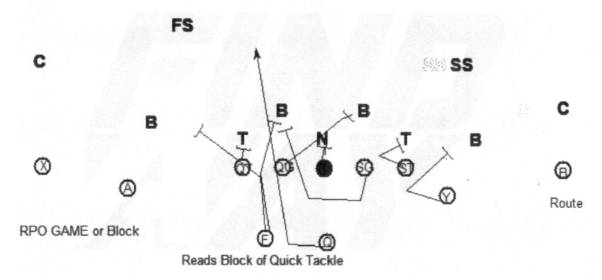

Position	Job Description
X	Same RPO's as in base
A	Same RPO's as in base
F	Lead on playside LB – Read block of the QT
Y	Gap - Hinge
B	Route Concept
QT	Block DE – Take where he wants to go
QG	Block #1 DL on playside of the center
C	On/Backside
SG	Pull Wrap – Eyes inside
ST	Gap - Hinge
Q	Slide step and downhill

Buck Pass

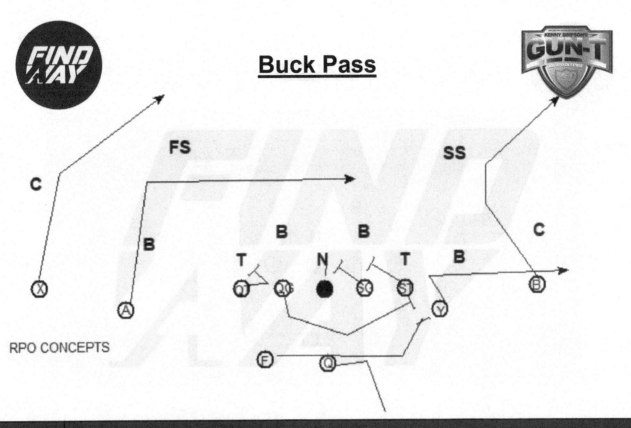

RPO CONCEPTS

Position	Job Description
X	Post over safety. If no safety, skinny post
A	Drag over linebackers
F	Fake buck, protect edge
Y	Down block for a count, then to the flats
B	Crack corner
QT	Rock/Load
QG	Rock/Load
C	Rock/Load
SG	Rock/Load
ST	Rock/Load
Q	Flash and drop shoulder pad level as you slide step. Read deep defender for high low. If DBs "spin" work to drag

Waggle

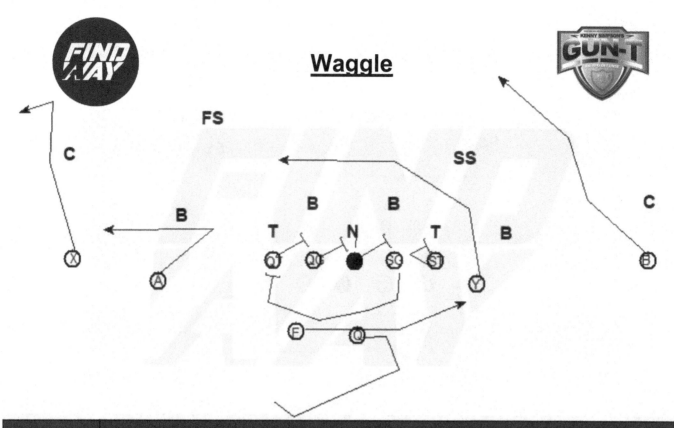

Position	Job Description
X	Smoke Route or Go Route
A	Whip Route
F	Fake buck, protect edge
Y	Drag Route
B	Post Over Safety
QT	Rock/Load
QG	Rock/Load
C	Rock/Load
SG	Rock/Load
ST	Rock/Load
Q	Fake and bucket step to gain depth and width – Reading Go-Whip-Drag

DUO
Base Rules

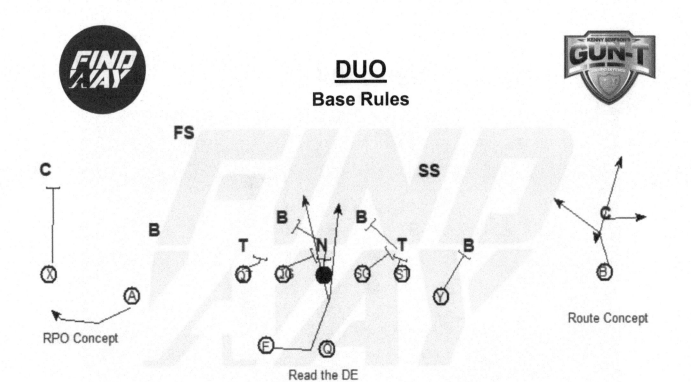

Position	Job Description
X	Same RPO's as in base
A	Same RPO's as in base
F	
Y	Lead on playside LB
B	Crack Safety or block corner if single high
QT	Step Hinge unless RPO
QG	Wrap to first daylight. Eyes inside
C	On/Backside
SG	#1 Defensive Lineman inside of the ST
ST	Block Out
Q	Same RPO's as in base

Quick Buck
Base Rules

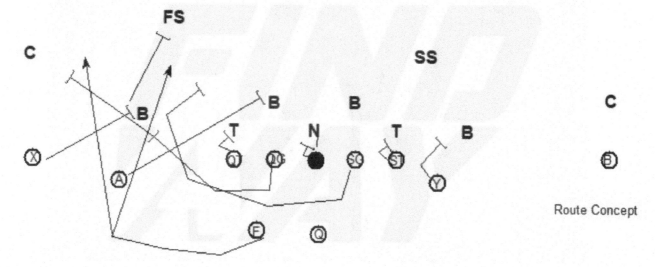

Route Concept

Position	Job Description
X	Crack OLB
A	Crack ILB
F	Swing and follow guards
Y	Gap Hinge
B	Route Concept
QT	Hook/Cut DE
QG	Pull kick/wrap
C	On/Backside
SG	Wrap to fist daylight. Eyes inside.
ST	Gap Hinge.
Q	If don't want the 1 on 1 route – throw swing to F.

Triangle

This is our wide bunch look. We will run most of our trips concepts from this set, but it causes a different strain on a defense due to the bunch set. Running any trips concepts from this look strains the defense.

This also is a good set for the screen game if you have physical WR's that are willing to block.   We have a few concepts we prefer from this set, but **any** part of the trips game is available from this.

Red
Lion Triangle

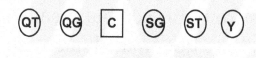

Position	Alignment
X	Top of the numbers
A	Outside shoulder of X. Off the ball.
F	Heels on QB toes. Split the QG and QT
Y	2 x 2 off ST.
B	Inside shoulder of X. Off the ball.
QT	Head even with hip of center. 2 ft splits
QG	Head even with hip of center. 2 ft splits
C	On Ball
SG	Head even with hip of center. 2 ft splits
ST	Head even with hip of center. 2 ft splits
Q	Heels at 5 yards

Blue
Triangle

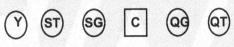

Position	Alignment
X	Top of the numbers
A	Outside shoulder of X. Off the ball.
F	Heels on QB toes. Split the QG and QT
Y	2 x 2 off the ST.
B	Inside shoulder of X. Off the ball.
QT	Head even with hip of center. 2 ft splits
QG	Head even with hip of center. 2 ft splits
C	On Ball
SG	Head even with hip of center. 2 ft splits
ST	Head even with hip of center. 2 ft splits
Q	Heels at 5 yards

Red Triangle
Belly-Fast

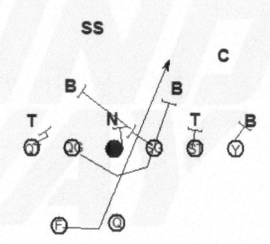

Position	Alignment
X	Block MDT
A	Fast Screen
F	Belly
Y	Block Out
B	Block Corner - MDT
QT	Step-Hinge
QG	Pull Wrap
C	On-Backside
SG	#1 First level defender to backside LB
ST	#2 First level defender
Q	Read Numbers – Or can read RPO

Red Triangle
Belly-Peak

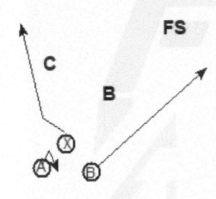
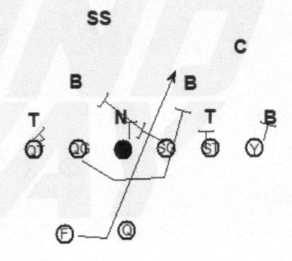

Position	Alignment
X	Go #s
A	Fast Screen
F	Belly
Y	Block Out
B	Peak
QT	Step-Hinge
QG	Pull Wrap
C	On-Backside
SG	#1 First level defender to backside LB
ST	#2 First level defender
Q	Read ILB

Red Triangle
Quick Belly - Bubble

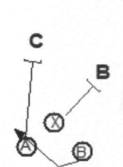

Position	Alignment
X	Block MDT
A	Block #1
F	Block for Quick Belly
Y	Step-Hinge
B	Bubble
QT	Block DE
QG	Quick Belly Rules
C	On-Backside
SG	Pull Wrap
ST	Step-Hinge
Q	Read #'s

Red Triangle
Quick Buck

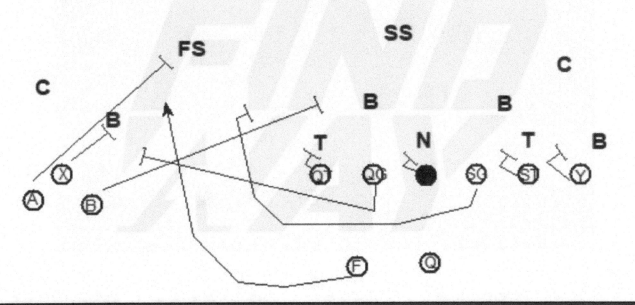

Position	Alignment
X	Crack
A	Crack
F	Quick Buck
Y	Step-Hinge
B	Crack ILB
QT	Block DE
QG	Pull Kick
C	On-Backside
SG	Pull Wrap
ST	Step-Hinge
Q	Toss

Red Triangle
Snag

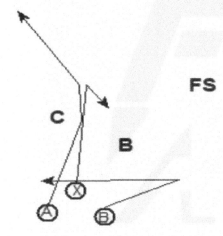
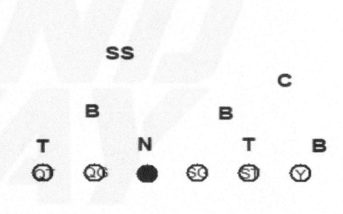

Position	Alignment
X	12-10 Curl
A	Crack - Corner
F	
Y	Step-Hinge
B	Whip Route
QT	
QG	
C	
SG	
ST	
Q	Same Read as Base – "SNAG"

Red Triangle
Flood

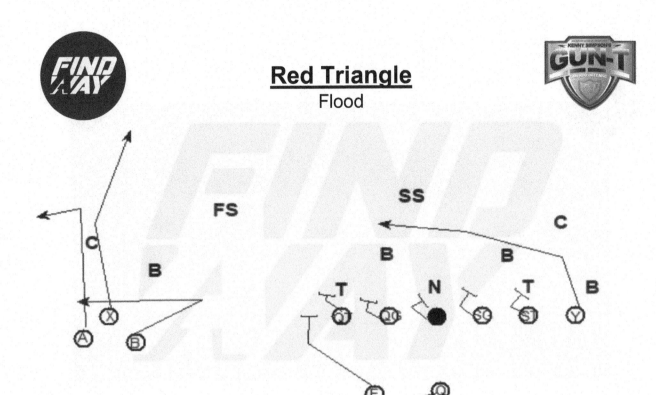

Position	Alignment
X	Skinny Post
A	15 – Out Route
F	
Y	Drag (if running Rodeo/Lasso)
B	Whip Route
QT	
QG	
C	
SG	
ST	
Q	Same Read as Base – "Flood"

 # Roar/Lion Flop

One way to adapt this offense to more of a 3-wide is to get into this set. Allowing the offense to keep a clear strong side and isolate our "A". This also allows for more "train" motion if your "A" is your better athlete than your "B".

A few different concepts to match personnel:

1) Train motion for Jet

2) Getting our "A" isolated for 1 on 1 routes

3) Getting a lighter box for base run plays

Red
Lion Flop

Position	Alignment
X	Top of the numbers
A	Top of the numbers off the ball
F	Heels on QB toes. Split the QG and QT
Y	Head even with hip of center. 2 ft splits
B	Split the difference. Toes on heels of X.
QT	Head even with hip of center. 2 ft splits
QG	Head even with hip of center. 2 ft splits
C	On Ball
SG	Head even with hip of center. 2 ft splits
ST	Head even with hip of center. 2 ft splits
Q	Heels at 5 yards

Blue
Roar Flop

Position	Alignment
X	Top of the numbers
A	Top of the numbers off the ball
F	Heels on QB toes. Split the QG and QT
Y	Head even with hip of center. 2 ft splits
B	Split the difference. Toes on heels of X.
QT	Head even with hip of center. 2 ft splits
QG	Head even with hip of center. 2 ft splits
C	On Ball
SG	Head even with hip of center. 2 ft splits
ST	Head even with hip of center. 2 ft splits
Q	Heels at 5 yards

Quick Buck
Base Rules

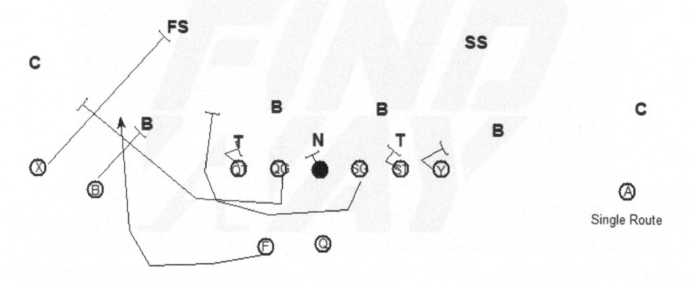

Single Route

Position	Job Description
X	Crack second level defender
A	Route Concept
F	Swing and follow guards
Y	Gap-Hinge
B	Crack 2nd level defender
QT	Hook/block down on/cut - DE
QG	Pull Kick
C	Cut first defender to playside
SG	Pull – Wrap first daylight – EYES INSIDE
ST	Gap-Hinge
Q	Take single route or throw swing

Train - Jet
Base Rules

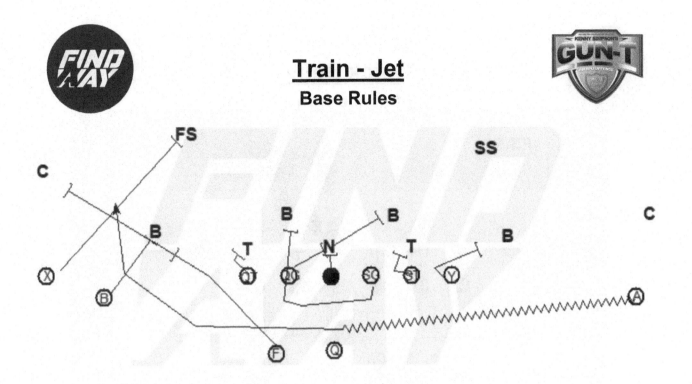

Position	Job Description
X	Crack 2nd level defender
A	Jet
F	Kick first defender that shows
Y	Gap - Hinge
B	Crack 2nd level defender
QT	Block DE – Take where he wants to go
QG	Block #1 DL on playside of the center
C	On/Backside
SG	Pull Wrap – Eyes inside
ST	Gap - Hinge
Q	Slide step and downhill

Quick Belly
"Influence with F"

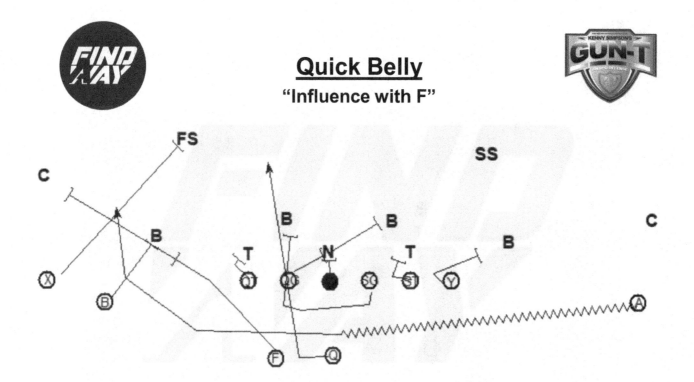

Position	Job Description
X	Crack 2nd level defender
A	Fake Jet
F	Can lead on LB – or can influence block
Y	Gap - Hinge
B	Crack 2nd level defender
QT	Block DE – Take where he wants to go
QG	Block #1 DL on playside of the center
C	On/Backside
SG	Pull Wrap – Eyes inside
ST	Gap - Hinge
Q	Slide step and downhill

Belly
Base Rules

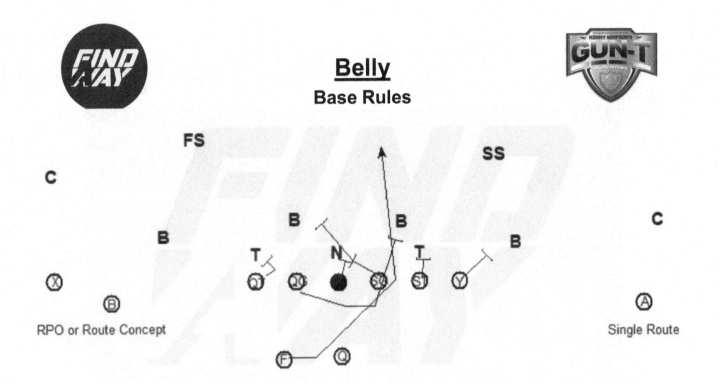

Position	Job Description
X	Same RPO's as in base
A	Route or crack
F	
Y	Block out
B	RPO concept
QT	Step Hinge unless RPO
QG	Wrap to first daylight. Eyes inside
C	On/Backside
SG	#1 Defensive Lineman playside
ST	#2 Defensive Lineman
Q	Same RPO's as in base

If – Then

Built in Answers

If-Then

One of the reasons this offense was developed was the premise of the Wing T – IF the defense does this, THEN the offense should do this…

This premise was also big in the RPO game – that is the reason it was invented – to place players in conflict. IF the defender does this, THEN the offense runs/passes.

In any offense this should be the thought process. Have built in adjustments ready to go. This offense was designed to have these built in to any play concept we install. Having these available should provide answers for whatever the defense throws at you.

Blending these two concepts together has been very helpful for calling plays. It keeps it clear and simple in most of the base play calls, not only for the coach, but for the athletes. Making sure they understand (especially the Quarterback) what will happen when the defense tries to take something away. In this section I plan to go over 5 "IF-THEN" concepts.

If-Then

IF the defense overloads to stop Buck Sweep…THEN the answers should be:

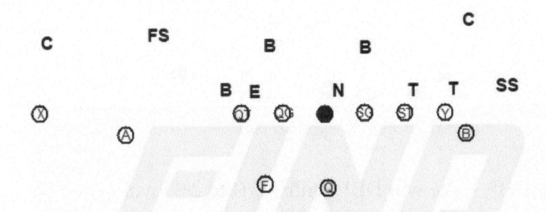

1) Belly – Block out on Defensive line and run underneath SS

2) Buck Pass – Read the corner for the shot play

3) B-Pop or X Crack and go – If corner is very aggressive make the read simple for your QB

4) Waggle – More than likely TE will come wide open in this look

5) RPO Game on the backside – Steal would be a good call here for QB pull. Could also just throw quick game depending on depth of DB's

6) Counter – Counter is also an option in this look

If-Then

IF the 9 technique is a big problem, THEN we will run a few concepts.

1) Bypass – We will send B to 2nd level and kick quickly

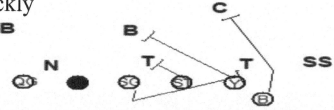

2) DBL – We will DBL with TE/B to 2nd level

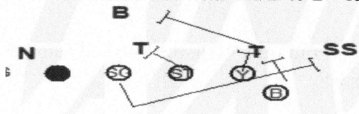

3) Belly and widen splits – Widen him out by alignment and run belly

4) Counter Read – If he is squeezing hard we will run counter with the QB and read the 9 technique

If-Then

IF the backside DE is crashing hard, THEN we will do the following:

1) Run "Steal" on strong side run game

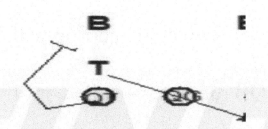

2) Run quick side plays – Quick buck, quick belly, counter should all hit much easier.

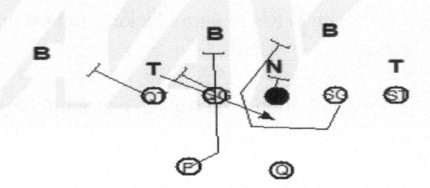

3) Fan block "quick belly"

If-Then

IF the defense is in man-0, THEN we will use the following concepts:

1) Lots of motion concepts

2) Squeeze formation and flop with crack calls

3) Run QB run game – called or off RPO reads

4) Screen game to the RB – identify who is covering and get him blocked

5) Crack with WR's to gain blockers and set up play action

6) Empty formations and trips to cause lighter boxes

If-Then

IF the Quarterback is struggling with RPO game, THEN use these concepts:

1) Play action game that looks like RPO

2) QB Runs that are designed

3) Signal when you want him to take the pass in some form

4) Roll him out of pocket to clean up the throw/read and use this as your RPO game

Conclusion

 # Conclusion

I want to thank you for your interest and support. As a coach it is challenging to "put yourself out there" for the coaching community and I have been humbled by those who have reached out. I've enjoyed getting to know coaches from all over the globe, and it is truly inspiring to see all those that are reaching and working with the future generations.

As a coaching getting older in our profession I try to close out all of my books/manuals by giving some advise that I have learned the hard way:

1) Remember this is a game. Compete and do everything in your power to help your team, but do not forget to teach them life lessons. Coaches have great influence, and if all we do is teach football, we are failing our players.

2) Don't get too complicated. Simple and fundamentally sound teams usually win. Creativity is fun, but do not neglect the basics.

 # Conclusion

3) Continue to develop and grow as a coach. Take something from this and other coaches. Use resources as much as you can. Each year we adapt and adjust and I take from others that have shown a great example. Be a lifelong learner.

For those of you interested:

The entire system can be found on Coachtube.com: https://bit.ly/GUNTRPOSystem

There is also more information on my website: FBCoachSimpson.com

Feel free to also reach out with questions: FBCoachSimpson@gmail.com

Coach Simpson
FindAWay

About The Author

Coach Simpson is currently the Head Football Coach at Searcy High School, a 6A school in Arkansas. Before taking the job at Searcy, Simpson was the Head Football Coach at Southside High School, a 4A school in Arkansas. Taking over a program that had won eight games in five seasons and had been on a 20+ game losing streak, Simpson has led Southside to the playoffs for four-consecutive seasons and won two conference titles in the past three seasons. For his efforts, he was named 4A-2 Conference Coach of the Year (2017), named to the as a finalist for Hooten's Coach of the Year (2017) and has been the All-Star Nominee for the 4A-2 (2016 and 2019).

This is Coach Simpson's 4th book. He was a best-selling author for his first work Find a Way: What I Wish I'd Known When I Became a Head Football Coach. The book was released in 2019 and is available on FBCoachSimpson.com. It has sold over 1800 copies as of 2020. This is also the 2.0 version of the GUN-T-RPO Playbook. The first book has already sold over 1000 copies in just 6 short months.

About The Author

Simpson also raised over $1.5 million for Southside during his 9 seasons and has overseen several major facility projects including: New Field Turf, Expansion to Fieldhouse, Expansion to the school's home bleachers, and the addition of a press box and a new video-board.

Prior to his time at Southside, Simpson was the Head Coach at Alabama Christian Academy in Montgomery, Alabama. During his tenure there, Simpson took over a team that had been 4-18 and led them to their first home playoff game in over 20-years. For his efforts he was named Montgomery Advertiser's All-Metro Coach of the Year as well as being voted 4A Region 2 Coach of the Year (2010). Simpson also served as the head track coach at ACA and led the girl's and boy's teams to multiple top 10 finishes in 4A.

About The Author

Simpson began his coaching career at Madison Academy, in Huntsville, Alabama. He served as a junior high basketball and football coach, before working into a varsity coaching role in football. He graduated from Harding University in 2003. He is married to Jamey and has three children: Avery, Braden and Bennett. The couple was married in 2001 after meeting at Harding University.

Contact Coach Simpson

@FBCoachSimpson – Twitter
Kenny Simpson – Facebook
FBCoachSimpson.com

Recommendations

 # Quotes

"Coach Simpson's Gun-T offense brilliantly merges the best aspects of the Wing T and the shotgun RPO offenses."
-Brian Garrett, Offensive Line Coach, Airline High School, Bossier City, LA

"After my second year as a head coach, I knew we needed to make a change from running a zone scheme. I began looking for something that could maximize our talent at all positions and came across Coach Simpson's system. As I began to look at his book, I knew this was the system for us. It marries easy to run traditional base plays with the more modern RPO systems of today. What's great about Coach Simpson's Gun-T system, is that it's easy to install and build off of. We were able to adopt multiple pass options off the base buck sweep. We also added variations of buck, counter and power with different players and motions, and still have pass options on the outside and across the middle of the field. Whether you've run the wing-T for a long time or are a traditional zone guy, if you're looking to adapt a new, easy to install system that your players will love, Coach Simpson's Gun Wing-T System will take your offense to a new level!"
-Derrick Elman, Head Football Coach, Humboldt Community School

 # Quotes

"Coach Kenny Simpson's book is top notch. We have been able to integrate some things into our offense as they relate to what we do already. We saw an instant upgrade in our run game and our players & staff were more confident that we could run the ball. Thank you for all you do for coaches."
-Anthony Johns, Offensive Coordinator, Valley Lutheran HS in Phoenix AZ